this
is
no
ordinary
rapture…

kerryn tredrea

© Paroxysm Press 2023

No part of this publication may be reproduced or transmitted in any form without the written permission of the publisher - apart from limited reproduction for the purposes of review, criticism or research as allowed under the Copyright Act 1968.

Paroxysm Press
PO Box 3107
Rundle Mall
Adelaide
5000
[Australia]

www.paroxysmpress.com
www.facebook.com/paroxysmpress
www.twitter.com/paroxysmpress
www.instagram.com/paroxysmpress
paroxysm@paroxysmpress.com

this is no ordinary rapture
Kerryn Tredrea
ISBN 978-1-876502-26-3

Cover art: Meg Wright (Red Wallflower Photography)

wild at heart.

dismounting the last train
to walk the secret paths of memory
and longing,
turning in circles around the real issue
which is forgetting.
and the moon will supervise the exorcism
as you laugh with the junkies and cry with the
saints when you know it should be the other way round,
but it's like walking up a really steep hill, or a
dingo, all you want is to be wild at heart.

the book of us.

the melting will happen
in the heat of your arms
where i will make it clear to you
with the arch in my back
and the clinging of my fingers
that the book of us
is yet to be written.

the melting will happen,
happen in space,
and in time.
this is not a journey
of the brain, we have a physicality
that lusts for something other,
that cries for relief
from the singular story.

right now distance
is our aphrodisiac
as we send out our proxies,
the surges that alert us
of this being no ordinary fiction
but a fact as solid as
the truth behind my eyes
and in my songs of yearning.

the melting will happen
and our appetites will be sated.

the melting will happen
and it will turn into our foundation.

the melting will happen.

the muse.

cut me deep with carnal knowledge
tear open my wounds, old and new
to find the vein of ashes i contain.
spill them on this page.

channel whatever thunderbolt it takes
to have me shaking with the rapture,
dancing above my earthly bonds and gravity
as my nightgown drips
with the extent of my levitation.

take the particular difficulties i face,
spike their dismembered heads
then mount them around our perimeter.
make me a cautionary tale.

follow the trail and find me silent,
fill me with your tindersticks for kindling
then strike the match that sparks the rage
that takes on this whole damn catastrophe.

any muse would choose me but i want you
with your wicked knowledge and gothic inclinations.
we have a smoldering love, a fire that tends
itself as i feed the wolves and howl for your attention.

although.

we find our happy place
parkbenching with coffee,
and although i don't expect it
we both end up crying.
it's not so much
the words you say as
the deep sense of
hopeful ennui
we both share.
we feel intrepid,
and although the heart
that you give me is
cracked and bloody
it is whole.

holding on.

i taste you
the next day
in my mouth,
feel you on my face,
memories scratched
skin to skin,
connections formed
in the heat where
science and chemistry
assist in our passion.

again
my ovaries call,
helping me find
the letting go,
the giving in.
i tell you it's a journey
so you show me
that you can hold on,
and you hold on to me.

easy prey.

it doesn't take much
a touch, a tender breath
for the completely inappropriate
not to matter, and for love,
or something like it
to sit on my worn out sofa,
stroke my hair and tell me
that the underside of everything
is easy prey, so we must press
our bellies together,
show our shells to the world
and edgewise find tomorrow.

swallow the stars.

turn a kiss into
something wicked,
make chemistry and desire
transpire to a time
of great flaming.

touch me roughly,
lock your fingers
to my flesh
in a way that is
frightening and
marvellous.

forge the chains
then break them
in a forgetting of
everything but lust.

take my breath away.

nothing can shake off
the dust but passion
will wash our mortality
to the bones. then
when all is raw and sated
we swallow the stars
and start again.

the small arrangements

we stay until
our shadows grow
so long
they are almost
out of reach.

you linger, touch my hand
and say "there
is just one
thing more…"

sound turns hollow
and the crickets weep
but our glory
will live in
the small arrangements.

the busker.

in a cage of non conformity she sits,
waits for the rain to pass and nods at
those who take the time to flick a smile
or toss a coin at her sun dried hat.
she sings her songs to the breath of her roots,
honouring her ancestors by educating
those who changed her country.

there is a history here too deep to fathom
in a glance, but its echos sound
down the colonnade and into laneways.
her voice fills the uninitiated with a yearning,
a dreaming of the old lands and times
when food was caught and eaten as a family
and the only real danger lay in not belonging.

her songs are a cry to the spirits that
inhabit us all, the long notes a thread
of connection to country. they speak to
the trees, to the grasses, to the rivers
and to the beasts, she sings to the shopgirls
and bar boys and business owners,
to her aunties and uncles and brothers
and sisters and most of all
she sings to her mother.

badlands.

the clay that i am made of
crumbles back into the landscape.
it's gully dry
and sunset will surely catch me,
wrap me in a blanket
of badlands hospitality.

this mother nature's cradle
is full of nettles and shale
but my boots keep moving,
through the badlands
through the undergrowth
which is the only growth
around these parts.

this glorious colour pallette
ain't gunna save me
when every road i walk on
keeps crumbling into dust.
i blend with the canyons
as distant mesas foreshadow
the way through
and it ain't no sin
to be glad to be alive.

ripped off #12 badlands (bruce springsteen)

tsunami.

it wasn't the white flash winter
we all expected in the 80s,
or the terrorists, as the hot flushes
rip and we're forced to watch
the apocalyptic film clip
wishing for an alternative ending.

serendipity shuns what it does
not understand with waves
that answer to no one. water
is not life, nature is not my
mother and now they tell me
the earth has shifted.

there's been a deep rift of spirits,
and everyone's left with muddy feet
as we gaze into the agonizing chasm,
surrendering to the waves of emptiness,
wishing for an alternative ending.

when the skies glow red.

don't breathe.
there is no oxygen left,
the fire has taken it all.

don't move,
there is no place
safe for humans.

you understand heat
but these hundred shades of hell
are so unnatural you wonder
which planet you've been moved to.

dryness tightens your skin
and liquid filters through you,
you're a sieve.
your brain screams "panic!"
but your heart cries "be careful."
how can anything survive this?
you think,
and then you try not to.

every horizon drops
and the atmosphere is
completely visceral,
specks of darkness fall
and you know they were once
living things, taken by the flame.

the light/dark paradox
of your situation is
ultimately eased by time
but somewhere something
is changed - you can never
unknow a fire.
you can survive it, or not
but mother nature is a dominating bitch
etching your psyche with her lessons.

so when the skies glow red,
then black
you'd better have
your buckets full
and your affairs in order.

for you, at two.

this is to you my little mirror gnome, strong and mighty,
unburdened now and chasing a life that excites you
and ignites everyone around you.

you are the seed and the farmer,
you are the beautiful flower,
you are wisdom and discovery,
you are history and the future.

you will learn the language of the seasons,
tie them up with your instincts to carry lightning in your veins.

you will fall in love with the moon nightly,
not to any prescription or code of honour
but from a faith so deep and mysterious it cannot be named.

on some sundays and during thunderstorms you will struggle
with insomnia, and monthly, always monthly you will be
reminded that life is a struggle, but you are strong.

affirm yourself often.

bang your own drum loudly
but listen out for other beats,
they will inspire you.

some days you will be singing in rainbows,
others are nothing but the blues.
celebrate both days with grace.

let the sound of distant buses be a dreaming
of possibilities that take you places.

don't fall for the fast laugh or the quick friendship,
worthy people take time and are the
framework on which to build yourself.

be loyal to your sisters, treat yourselves
with respect then everybody else will.

aim always to be better than yesterday.

dream in architecture, dream in riddles,
dream under sunshine and in the halflight.
dream in truths, dream in solutions,
dream for your own amusement then
dream for the entertainment of the world.

i wish you to speak the profound
and run with wild abandon.
i want you to be proud, stake your claim,
hold boldness in your heart and in your hands.
then when all around you is madness i want you
to come to me and be your own kind of crazy,
i can say "i understand"
because we are family.

good speed son.

hanging with elemental boy,
stretch till it hurts
(it always hurts, but
that's his lesson to learn).
then he navigates
a different passage,
wrangling the unruly stallion
into understanding.

straddled in the middle world
where black and white
turn murky grey while
gazing at the miasma
of adulthood.
he knows there are things
he doesn't want to know
but cant stop wanting them.

he teaches me
my boundaries
and inconsistencies,
reflecting me in a way
that terrorizes and amazes.
he amazes me constantly
and we love
the story so far.

the debono poems.

yellow.

he was not the messiah
but the message he spread
was so yellow with hope,
so full of yeasty supposings
that he bought everyone to
critical mass,
and the tipping point.
let the stars guide him
safely, as the earthly
murmurs don't hold
their power in the face of
such logic and love. he is here
so the globe of the world sits
better on all our shoulders.

black.

as she looks deep and sighs
she can see the dangers
in dark shadows,
knows the traps
of both roads travelled.
still she slowly guides
the blindfolded through
the black perils, alerting
the melancholic night birds
that it is always
five minutes to midnight.

red.

in a quiet night light
or in a tempest/
with a sense that
isn't literal/
when you're addicted to
the adrenalin of panic/
you witness mishaps
and disturbing practices/
that are wicked
and vicious/ so
you find good reasons
for bad blood/
hide in the red/
in which you feel
the infinite.

green.

she felt as though her head
was pregnant, so fertile
with ideas she could have
birthed a dynasty.
she was always two steps ahead,
or behind, or outside,
finding new ways to amaze
as the word orgasms poured
over green weaknesses
and greener strengths.
maternal to the end she vows
in a whisper that she will be
always be there
to hear you roar.

white.

he took an outside view
with any in-crowd, ignoring
the cinematic demons
behind his eyes he
filled his head with numbers,
quantified life in a
new - white - order
to find his place with
the creatives. sometimes
there was an absence
of something, a dried
raindrop, but it was
his destiny to become
the ballast to weather
any storm.

blue.

we are not formed by
angels but the more time
we spend in the sky, flying
through blue perspectives,
injecting the discovery
of the seasons we
dismantle the ego
to embrace the whole
keen city.
we go far from the subliminal
world of yesterday and the
maybe promises of
tomorrow, we shun
unexplained metaphors
for the power heavy
pendulum of knowledge
and compassion.

tribute.

the blackbird of unhappiness
lays dead on my feet,
shot with lithium
and other feelgood drugs.
it's written like a habit
all over your face.

your tunes ride on
the ties that bind
so inspired by crime that
kylie had to die
for nick to hit the mainstream.
i love you like coffee,
you make me so edgy.

you caught me maintaining
my secrets on a leash,
wearing your songs
like wet socks on a dismal day
(ringo starr in the minor key)
because you can feign sadness,
but you can't pretend togetherness.

so tell me i'm beautiful again
while i play morrissey music
till there is no tomorrow
just you
and me
and his words
    killing me softly with a blunt object.

self reflection.

i accused mean mr. mustard
in the conservatory,
with the whips and chains.
but the backlash is severe
on my fledgling hump when he says
"no one knows what love is!"
when you're vicious pretty
the gymp suit never comes off.

i find my window of opportunity
and look through to the red light district.
but i've forgotten my green eye shadow
so not even the whores will accept me.
in a place where stranger and danger kiss
images of childhood nightmares play out
and it's ok to use sins of the past
as tools of the present.
end of opening montage.

the ants have arrived early
to find me clutching at scarecrow straws
and howling at the moon.
but it's really the thrill of the spilled blood
and the side effects of the egg donation
reeking havoc in my body and
even in a rerun melodrama it's still
too early to return to the scene of the crime.

in no man's land. "cocktails or slumbershades?"
flashbacking tragedies and
snatching morsels of affection.
but tomorrow is polly wally tuesday
in the united states of unrelentless
so smash the bulbs boys
cos I'm more afraid of the light than the dark.
i may dance naked in front of the mirror
but I have no time for self reflection.

this is a slam poem.

this is not a slam poem,
it's not a love poem either,
i'm not trying to sweep you away.
this poem made me reach for
a knife and not a pen to write it.

this is not a slam poem.
it's not a warm handshake either.
i'm very nervous you know
so this may all be a clammy delirium.

this poem has the expectations of a fire extinguisher.

this is not a slam poem.
it's not an occasion for self congratulation either,
what am i going to say to myself?
bravo, you're not dead...?
no, i've got the stage and i say
fuck the world and fight on punks.

this poem carries its stuff around in broken suitcases.

this poem was written at bus stops and
in the supermarket, where i am edgy
and indecisive. some parts,
the brighter parts
were written outside
in the sunshine
while i was looking at trees.

this poem is well into its third trimester.

this poem is a tenuous blending
of me and my persona, and
although it may be one rung up
from bedlam i can see
the poetry of mapping the moon
with my eyes, misusing my manners
and mopping up my own muddy footprints.

this poem was written with more need than want.

this poem was written because this moment is all we have.

this poem accepts its punishment.

this is a slam poem.

distance.

at the edge of the brave stage,
the water's fine.
"come in" he said
by way of invitation,
waving his hand at normal.

"but the water,
it comes and goes…"
untroubled by the
fragility of nature
the others crowd around
the rock pool,
content to paddle.

always too far
they say,
waving.

fragile.

they met in a land of missed connections
in the year of bad timing.
he came from the clouds or
the mountains, high on expectations
but jangling with tambourine dreams
and too much energy.
she revealed herself one sentence at a time.

he was never still but very deep,
so deep she stuck to the shallows
for fear of drowning. "i'm not used
to travelling such long distances"
she said, making him ache in places
he had been ignoring for a long time too.

the laws of nature are elusive, so
when they danced, they danced to music
with a strong melody line, and an
irregular beat. and when he fell apart
she patched him up, but the pieces were
deeply broken, some left behind with
old friends, in pawn shops and in
cemeteries, so she never really found him.

and when it wasn't easy she grew hard,
falling again into a well of bad habits. while
he searched in vain for a lifeline all he
found were more needles.
there was some suspicion of a demons plot,
but forgetting the rhetoric she tucked him
under a cautious blanket, on the longest night
and pretending the ease of an opera diva
watched the closing credits roll.

courting fever.

courting fever
like it may choose
another over me
he fulfills my wishes,
taking me to a
fetid dreamscape
where it is
dank tropical.
dark clouds fill
my periphery
as i float
on refraction,
glide through time,
deaf to everything but
the crackling intensities.
i am wracked
with unbidden explosions
as i fall into the
broiling cauldron.
begging for relief i
just cannot seem
to let you go

twenty seven.

my lover said
"coffee is bad
for your heart
my darling."
selfish bastard.
we both sit
and watch
my mortality drip
through the filter
and everything has
the smell of coffee
about it
and the feeling of
a biting snake,
sharp
and to the point.

howl if you must.

take me on that tangent
that you go on,
the one where we mount
trusted steeds
to ride the high streets
shouting "fuck the world!"
and other noble insults.

take me to the place
where everything is natural,
where we fill up on spinach
and the wonder of the stars,
pitch rocks into unfathomably
deep holes and in nearly
diabolical thinking, strip our skins
so we can be truly naked.

take me now, while we're dancing.
you choose the music
while i play something
sexy and evil.
within this skin
lie the secrets of the visceral,
i drag them out
and lay them at your table.

take me here, where the mercies
that you seek must be fought for,
muscles must melt and
beasts must bay at the moon
before this is finished -
it is an irresponsible sky
that watches over
our dark acts.

take me to the brink as
the whole darkness
consumes us.
sink your talons deep
into my breast, for my
sweet meats lie within.
show no sorrow,
plunge deep to scoff
upon my entrails
before the palsy happens.

take me to the point where
i am tipping.
wicked is the sin that trips us
when all i feel is
st. vitus dancing
up my spine and our loins
explode with truth serum
to leave us dripping
with significance.

waiting for the mania – a villanelle for michael.

elements of schizophrenia appear in my behaviour,
distant thunder trumpets an omen of a closer armageddon
and the saviour of our souls has lost his way.

since you went flying without me i cry unsad tears
at irrelevant moments while the true grief goes unmourned.
elements of schizophrenia appear in my behaviour.

i suffer a loss of consciousness due to the bastardisation
of the documentary form that is reality television,
and the saviour of our souls has lost his way.

st. john whispers in my ear, trying to defend himself
but his whining irritates and i break out in a rash.
elements of schizophrenia appear in my behaviour.

sylvia did it one year in ten, turned it all into a
circus, then stood too close to the lion's breath,
and the saviour of our souls has lost his way.

and the answer seems to be in the skies (sun blind and
scared of the dark, you went flying without me).
elements of schizophrenia appear in my behaviour,
and the saviour of our souls has lost his way.

earthquakes.

he is the epicentre of the earthquake in my bed
timber stiff he shakes the base of our whole relationship,
i wake in fright to the rocking of the naked marble man.

spitting vivid pictures over heartache covered floorboards,
tilting over the edge of everything, manipulating sorrow.
he is the epicentre of the earthquake in my bed.

my own nightmares quieten, my vampires hover
and the judgemental dead snigger their noses into their hands.
i wake in fright to the rocking of the naked marble man.

in the dark we fuck hellishly to fight off black fantasies
but when the quiet comes and the devil jacks his brain
he is the epicentre of the earthquake in my bed.

only the shadows know and they're not telling
what satan's song it is to make him dance this way,
i wake in fright to the rocking of the naked marble man.

the light switch breaks the spell but i'm still held
in the sweet and sour voice of the unattainable,
he is the epicentre of the earthquake in my bed
i wake in fright to the rocking of the naked marble man.

the nature of ghosts.

the back beats
of my depression
are the cello
and the knife...

        i'm having
        dagger in the back
        fantasies again

            because

                it is the nature
                of ghosts
                to not remain
                buried.

a lesson from the dead.

they have closed
the coffee shop
where you
committed suicide,
drinking cup
after cup
after cup
of coffee
too strong for
your heart
to handle.

i walk past,
trying to remember
the good times,
the sane times.
i flick my eyes
to the skies
because i don't
know where else
to look for you.

time does help
but cannot hold
my heart
the way that
you did,
like a badge
on your chest.
i still take
my coffee strong
as a lesson from the dead.

a thought is not an instinct.

pushing back the edges of depression – it's a quick-sand of insanity and i want to scream out "no!" but quickly the sand fills my mouth and i am drawn down into a deep and genuine paralysis of ennui. a thought is not an instinct.

blind. finding my level like water that creeps up to my nostrils in the night when there's nobody watching. my other senses are heightened, but not high enough for me to climb out of here. a thought is not an instinct.

the angry cello of depression strikes a chord in my gut like a cat climbing the curtain of a burning ship while the orchestra keeps on playing, keeps on playing, the angry cello keeps on playing. a thought is not an instinct.

howl. till i'm tearing up photographs and dancing with the moon. crippled kittens and limp spirits join in wanting excess and everything that goes with it so i light up a cigarette to shut out the rain. a thought is not an instinct.

the limits of elasticity.

moon crow delirious
coming up for air,
fighting survival
is not suicide
but another, darker place.

cracked land scares me
with its back breaking
potential, and even elastic
has its limits.

it is a landscape
of other stories
outside of my window
where joining in
is metered out
as to avoid suspicion.

there are gaping holes
that require covering,
pending rationalisations
that grow teeth
over time.
in laying it all
at my feet
the ground becomes
unsteady.

cigarettes & speed don't work any more.

dancing with dali in stocking'd feet.
he puts his hand up my skirt
then is appalled by the blood
(running like teardrops)
he finds there.
soft clocks watch
my everyday activities
but what more can i expect?
when nirvana is just
a flash of maybes.

having coffee with freud in all the wrong places.
he wants to sort out my
intimacy issues until i say
"old habits die hard, but
i will happily lay them out
and sleep
with their
corpses."
and the clouds, pregnant with rain,
wait for him to run.

linking arms with jesus cos he's the only one with clean needles.
he follows my lead, feeding
the ghosts, we say "hi" to
the guys that
we know.
the lap and slap of the river's edge
as erotic as an invitation
to cunnilingus, but he's like me
and prefers illusion to despair.
cigarettes & speed don't work any more.

idaho.

why is suicide so sexy
on the page
or in legends
but when our children are
necking themselves
my guts weaken
and my brow grows cold?

why are junkies
so cool in the movies,
so tragically beautiful,
so knowingly needy
but when one's dying in my bed
i just want to scream
and scream
and scream?
and there's not enough
washing powder
to scrub my linen clean.

and the bile that i spill
on the page, on the stage
does nothing to cleanse,
just adds to the collective
woe and knowing
that shaping my thoughts
into words does not make
them any more palatable.

being talked down
by the soothing tones of
john malkovich's speech
impediment i realise that
love is not the answer,
nor is pain,
just acceptance,
acceptance and hope.

chances are.

i've been cleaning the house up slowly, preparing for... armageddon? my doctor says i should view this new development more positively, and despite the obvious paradigm shift i do consider the diagnosis for a moment. but then the beat poets whisper in my ear through the aid of modern technology telling me we are all merely mammals, all eat, shit, crave, love, lose. i'd like to think i carry their flame or at least a spark of it but until i stick it under a spoonful of goof ball juice or sleep rough i am just a pretender.

i take my battle to the page where recycled words turn full circle to bite me in the tender parts and i am trampled by my best intentions. but grouping my thoughts does not make them any more television so i have to find the freedom in ripping on the page where nothing really matters. we've all cleaned up broken glass before, where temptation sits glinting, asking the question, daring you to answer.

i want to speak secrets locked up in vaults, dry truths that blow dust under closed doors and down cul de sacs. i want to run with the lions in cites dangerous, chew up my shoes in parts unknown. i want to clear out the dander of shelves full of notebooks to find just the right word for every occasion. i want to break free of the place where grieving is a noun and not a verb. i am not a grief, i grieve and then i am done.

and although i am often beyond the pale the grip of addiction still splits me with a force as hard as good and evil, as powerful as yes and no. so i'm hanging with the hedonists and too timid to commit to the spirituality of it, but behind my eyes and in my synapses there's a crackle with the possibilities of another lifestyle, another talent, another virtue. chances are...

before sunrise

before sunrise
there is a serenity
and no confusion.
i wake
absorbing the calm,
walk outside where
the nightbirds are losing
their melancholia.

the air
is harder to breathe
because everything good
must be fought for.
the atmosphere
tightens my skin
as the sky lightens
and opens an embrace
to the potential.

one day the heavens
will affirm my wishes,
one day the moon
will bring me home.
i reach for the sky
not to surrender
but to contain
the amazing.

desperately seeking vertebrates.

human jellyfish adrift in a septic ocean
flood my inbox with toxic notes
regarding affirmation.
i reply in svengali,
my natural language
that my affirmations are my own
   i rise to the occasion
   i rise to the occasion
   i rise to the occasion
and the oceans i seek are deep and blue,
true to the moon and the rhythms of my body.
being semantic sea creatures i thought they'd
understand, but by the time the translations
have been made their interest is lost
and they float off to the next safe harbour.

shifting gears to
another state of mind
the two wolves inside me,
all teeth and hackles,
fighting over
   "should i?"
collapse into the comfort of his arms,
   or "shouldn't i?"
when i look into his eyes it's always midnight.

sitting at the table
in shades of hallelujah
take me to the river,
shake me like a pentecostal,
forgive me the pain of my own humanity
and birth me a picture of
happily ever after.

prince valiant arrives anyway
wearing the safety colour
and the scent of elsewhere.
he has the darkest
eyes i can imagine,
asylum eyes,

lupine and vulnerable
and i cant help but want to
run with his pack.
    i've been thinking about you and what you did last night.
    i've been thinking about you and what you did last night.
    i've been thinking about you and what you did last night.

having a soft spot for hard men
i fall for the same arsehole
again and again.
i carry a small bald guy
around in my pocket,
rub his head sometimes
in the hope of better fortune.
    i've been thinking about you and what you did that night.
    i've been thinking about you and what you did that night.
    i've been thinking about you and what you did that night.

i'm on a full mood mood swing,
you know, that time of the month when
you make dogs behave badly
and the truth demons are
banging on your door,
baying for your blood.
but they're not smart enough
to break down my barriers
reinforced with rationalisations.
even so,
there are some songs i cant sing in my head
for fear that
i may never come out.

i read it in the papers, it scared the shit out of me.
i read it in the papers, it scared the shit out of me.
i read the news today, oh boy,
    it really scared the shit out of me.

awake at 3 a.m.

awake at 3 a.m.
mainlining the soft
porn content of the
ab swing commercial.

awake at 3 a.m.
crawling into the refuge
of the the unholy trinity of
coffee, cones and codeine.

awake at 3 a.m.
there are dangers
in this forest.

reaching down the throat
of my dreams i find that
patience is not a virtue
but a psychotic vortex
where there is no satisfaction.

i sift through the details
of previous conversations
looking for clues,
but the words fall too quickly
and the meaning is lost
so all i'm left with
is this gritty feeling.
awake at 3 a.m.

only the good.

it was a very poetic moment
as she raised the frying pan
above her head,
bared her teeth
and swung balletic with
such momentum
he could swear this time
she would actually, finally
take flight.

it was a familiar dance,
where he would read
a thousand nightmares
in her eyes while
she spewed profanities
and lashed out at the world,
a screaming banshee.
in a theatre of war
she would have been a major general.

the battle, he knew
was inside her head,
private, not for him to fight.

so he retrieves her
tiny frame from the floor,
plants kisses on her forehead
and tells her the only war cry he knows.
"only the good die young baby".
and hopes like hell
that it isn't true.

dancing in damnation.

beyond belief
is where you send me
into the flames
is where i wanna go
i've danced with the devil
and his will is strong boy
i'm dancing
i'm dancing
i'm dancing in damnation.

it isn't fair
and it isn't love
and it isn't blessed
by the lord above
so let's get carnal
let's get raw
we're dancing
we're dancing
we're dancing in damnation.

tomorrow isn't talking
and the past has had its say
we need a new religion
to keep the bad at bay
we're dancing
we're dancing
we're dancing in damnation.

it's like we're almost perfect
when we dance around this way.

the bitch card.

i'd rather sail the void
than swim it,
rather dance with devils
than meet them in the park,
i'd rather walk away from the fight
than bring it,
rather burn from both ends
than live life in the dark.

i'd rather plan the revolution
than use it,
rather play my own game
than sticking to the rules,
i'd rather find a pot of gold
than lose it,
rather burn my bridges
than hang around with fools

i'd rather play the bitch card
than let the fuckers win,
rather take my chances
on one almighty spin,
yes i'm throwing all my chances
on one almighty spin.

i'd rather live a good life
than fake it,
rather have my heart ripped out
than get down on my knees,
i'd rather give you everything
than take it,
i'd like to help you neighbourboy
but you're just so hard to please.

i'd rather play the bitch card
than let the fuckers win,
rather take my chances
on one almighty spin,
yes i'm throwing all my chances
on one almighty spin.

the wuthering.

there is a forever that lies in destiny,
a cold temper.
i have been here forever,
wiley, windy.
          (heathcliff, cathy, come home)

i am the sound of your childhood,
a sonata for sleepless nights
weaving a semi incestuous tale
set in a dark, dank world
lit with candles and desire.
          (heathcliff, cathy, come home)

i let the sunshine come
but softly, and sometimes,
and then i bring the wuthering
to rip through your guts
like the slice of the knife
and you just cannot seem
to find your way home.
          (heathcliff, cathy, come home)

windows keep you from each other
but not from the nightmares,
bad dream madness that reduces
you to capes in the night.
and only the earth can put it right
only death can unite this unholy coupling.
          (heathcliff, cathy, come home)

you think that love is noble
but i am black crow sick.
i am the tempest, hot and greedy,
and it is a poisoned morning
that makes me take you,
ripping across your trembles and sighs
to make them wrack every damn window.
          (heathcliff, cathy, come home)

i can give you moments,
but not years,
i can give you forever,
but not now.
love will lift you up
but the devil drags you
down to me.
        (heathcliff, cathy, come home)

ripped off #3 wuthering heights (kate bush)

yeah we all felt good.

following the circus of dirty romance
young, raw and free
we would shoot through highway veins
and live the black tar lifestyle
where far away is never far enough.

hell bent and holding distance in our hands
we owned nothing but my harpoon
and bobby's song.
with nothing left to lose we were doing something,
we were moving.
we both played hard till
bobby got the blues so bad
the only way out was to sing it.

we sought the road like drugs,
like bad advice.
holding hands and killing time
it wasn't til we found a ride
that bobby really shone.
yeah we all felt good when
bobby sang the blues.

celebrating our victories
at truck stop diners
from st. louis to cedar city
we'd strip our skins in parking lots
beside the road that keeps on glinting.
then the skies opened up and
we were pushing anything
to bring comfort to the pain.

but i kept getting nasty
as we headed down the line,
chasing a hit that wasn't there.
we thought we were free, but
we were slaves to each other,
and love, and the byways.
then when bobby couldn't take it
the road took bobby away
leaving me chasing the horizon

in a pursuit that never ends.

yeah, we all felt good when
bobby sang the blues.

still, on cold, wet nights i pull out my bandana,
kiss my harp and call out bobby's name.

yeah we all felt good when bobby sang the blues.

ripped off #5 me and bobby mcgee (kris kristofferson)

canary.

i am your canary,
you utter one sentence
and i am caged, ready
to go underground.
you send me deep
into the dark recesses
of your subconscious.

clumsily, carefully
i stumble
to the place where you can
talk about the demons, where
i am the silent witness
to the battles that you fight.
clumsily, carefully
you watch my face
to know when you are
digging too deep.

then when we can't hold
our breath any longer
you pull me up,
press your lips to mine
so that we can forget the
subterranean nightmare.
you can't go there unguarded
so i am your canary.

ripped off #15 canary in a coal mine (sting)

bill.

it's five minutes to midnight
and i'm taking a clown's advice,
it's laced with ennui and cynicism
and dick jokes that
we can both laugh at.

i buy him a meal because
i can see that he has been crying,
and over his black coffee steam
he tells me to abandon the tightrope
and hitch myself to a carny
cos the best any of us
can expect is mud.

outside the world remains
ringleader distant, and it's late but
there is still news to deliver.
i promise to plant mushrooms
on his grave so he can carry on
entertaining the living.

we become a rope.

lust tugs
at my edges
and my corners,
bursts through
my dreams
and my fantasies.

you are here
because i bring you,
because of who you are.

touch me
lick me
take me places
fill my spaces
because you
are goodness,
you carry the light
that might just
save me from
falling into the abyss
     but i don't want to talk
     about the vortex.

look for me
find me
it's never easy
but holding
onto hope,
clinging to each other
and our dreams
is a worthy journey,
then we become a rope.

this kind of chaos.

the manic ant creatures
are dancing to bowie
even though they don't know it.

the clouds are dancing too
but faster, on parade,
i know they're going further
than i have permission to ride.

the possibility of dancing
strikes me as funny, until
bowie hits my hips
and outside, in the sunshine
is the only place in the world,
and dancing, with abandon
can answer many questions.

it is just this kind of chaos
that draws the endorphins,
a relief full of irregular beats
and right now i'm a puppet to life,
and bowie, and dancing.

resurrection

i have this prevailing image
of a woman sinking.
it's not me,
she has a patch on one eye
and very bad teeth.
or maybe it is.

she seems to me stoic
but broken.
she looks like she has seen some shit
tried to come out swinging
but they took it out of her,
she lost her it.

it comes to me sometimes
that maybe she is my
cautionary tale.
perhaps i am her but my vision
is only half there.
there is a delicate prediction
of resurrection in her
one good eye,
there is a strength in the
set of her chest
that empowers her shoulders
and suggests
she is not finished.
we will rise again.

but this is no ordinary rapture.

meaning spans mystery but
not far enough
so we are always left
wondering there truth sits
and where we do.
meanwhile, it doesn't go
unnoticed by either of us
that by living the nomadic
lifestyle you never bore
anybody, but then again,
where does it end?

layers cannot cover
what is really needed
which is an unfolding,
an opening to the moment.
we try to patch
our ragged bones
and agree
that the minotaurs will
always be lurking,
but as a fear
and not a threat.

when i am with you
we are plunging the divine,
immersing ourselves in
the sheer white light
of our connection.
then when the rapture comes,
and it will come
we will drink with
long and gorgeous thirsts,
throw off our burdens
and dance.

Kerryn Tredrea writes about lust, madness, loneliness and connection as if they were the same thing. Tethered to her distinctive voice is a poetry donning worn-out doc martins keeping step with junkies, the poet insisting i find my window of opportunity / and look through to the red light district. Her style is consistent, and as she recognises risk-taking and mistake-making as a part of life, she comes out a sage: everything has / the smell of coffee / about it / and the feeling of / a biting snake, / sharp / and to the point.

– Heather Taylor-Johnson

www.ingramcontent.com/pod-product-compliance
Lightning Source LLC
Chambersburg PA
CBHW010021130526
44590CB00047B/3793